MATH MASTERS ANALYZE THIS!

Ratios and Rates Reasoning

Melanie Alvarez

Educational Media

rourkeeducationalmedia.com

Scan for Related Titles and
Teacher Resources

Before & After Reading Activities
Level: W

Before Reading:

Building Academic Vocabulary and Background Knowledge

Before reading a book, it is important to tap into what your child or students already know about the topic. This will help them develop their vocabulary, increase their reading comprehension, and make connections across the curriculum.

1. Look at the cover of the book. What will this book be about?
2. What do you already know about the topic?
3. Let's study the Table of Contents. What will you learn about in the book's chapters?
4. What would you like to learn about this topic? Do you think you might learn about it from this book? Why or why not?
5. Use a reading journal to write about your knowledge of this topic. Record what you already know about the topic and what you hope to learn about the topic.
6. Read the book.
7. In your reading journal, record what you learned about the topic and your response to the book.
8. After reading the book complete the activities below.

Content Area Vocabulary
Read the list. What do these words mean?

comparison
denominator
determine
equivalent
numerator
quantity
resulted
scrumptious
versions
vise versa

After Reading:

Comprehension and Extension Activity

After reading the book, work on the following questions with your child or students in order to check their level of reading comprehension and content mastery.

1. What are ratios? (Summarize)
2. What is one of the most important facts to remember when working with ratios? (Infer)
3. How many ways can you write ratios? (Asking questions)
4. What is the definition of proportion? (Text to self connection)
5. What is a unit rate? (Asking questions)

Extension Activity

Practice all the concepts in the book to master ratios and rates reasoning!

Table of Contents

Ratios in the Kitchen

Get ready for math to invade your kitchen!
Let's say you are baking a cake for your best friend's birthday. You want to use your grandmother's recipe for the perfect yellow cake.

Let's look at that recipe:

½ cup (113 g) butter

1 ½ cups (193 g) sugar

3 large eggs

2 ¼ cups (288 g) all-purpose flour

1 teaspoon (5.69 g) salt

3 ½ teaspoons (17.5 g) baking powder

1 ¼ cups (294.74 mL) milk

1 teaspoon (4.93 mL) vanilla

Sounds **scrumptious**, right? Well, you decide to add extra sugar to it, because you love sweets.

Your cake comes out of the oven, cools off, and you take a taste. Pffff! You have to spit it out. That sure doesn't taste like Grandma's perfect yellow cake.

What are Ratios?

Why do you think the cake did not taste good? Here's why: RATIOS. A ratio is a **comparison** of two quantities using division. There are many ratios in Grandma's recipe for yellow cake. The ratio of sugar to eggs, flour, butter, and the other ingredients is a set amount in the recipe.

A Famous Ratio:
Pi, or π, is the ratio of a circle's circumference to its diameter (c/d). That means if you divide the circumference of any circle by that circle's diameter, you will always get the ratio pi. Pi is substituted with 3.14 (an estimate) in many formulas, because the real decimal equivalent to pi has an infinite number of digits! Mathematicians have already discovered 13.3 trillion digits of pi!

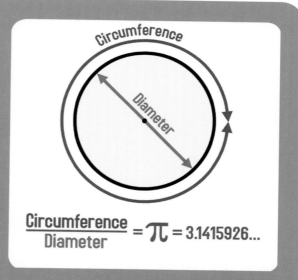

$$\frac{\text{Circumference}}{\text{Diameter}} = \pi = 3.1415926...$$

This is because bakers, like your grandmother, found that this amount of sugar compared to the amounts of the other ingredients in the cake **resulted** in the tastiest cake.

Once you added extra sugar to the cake, you changed the ratio of sugar to the other ingredients. The texture and taste became different. This is why bakers write those perfect ratios down as recipes. Bakers want to perfect the art of baking by creating their own signature RATIO for baking a yellow cake.

Reading and Writing Ratios

There are a few ways to write a ratio correctly. Let's take the example of three apples to two bananas.

One of the most important facts to remember when working with ratios is that order matters. Apples come first in the ratio, so you must keep them first, no matter which format you use.

You can write ratios in three ways:

Apples : Bananas

3 to 2 (using the word "to" to compare)	3 : 2 (using a colon to compare)	3/2 (written as a fraction to compare)

You try! Write the following as ratios in all three formats:

Practice A: **five** strawberries to **seven** blackberries

—— **to** —— —— **:** —— —— **/** ——

Practice B: **two** walnuts to **five** pieces of chocolate

—— **to** —— —— **:** —— —— **/** ——

All ratios can be written as fractions, but not all fractions are ratios. Fractions compare parts to a whole; ratios compare parts to a whole, wholes to other wholes, and parts to other parts.

One correct way to read ratios is by reading the colon or fraction bar as the word "to." You can also think of them read as "per" or "for every."

part/part	part/whole	whole/whole

Here are three types of ratio comparisons:

- **Part to part:** compares different parts of a group to each other (example: in a bowl of 25 grapes, 15 red grapes to 10 green grapes)

- **Part to whole:** compares one part of the group to the whole group (example: in a bowl of grapes, comparing 15 red grape to 25 total grapes)

- **Whole to whole:** compares one whole group to another whole group (example: 25 grapes for every 5 people)

For example:

The ratio of candies to cupcakes is 5:1.

5:1 (or 5/1) can be read as
"five candies per one cupcake"

or as

"five candies for every one cupcake"

or as

"five candies to one cupcake"

Equivalent Ratios and Proportions

Ratios are comparisons. Proportions are two **equivalent** (equal) ratios written with an equal sign between them. Suppose you are making fruit salad for a party. If you decide that you need more fruit salad for your guests, then you may want to double your recipe. This can be expressed as a proportion.

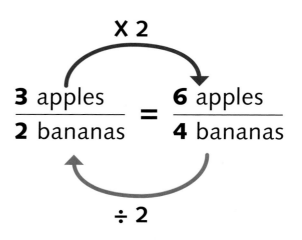

$$\frac{\textbf{3} \text{ apples}}{\textbf{2} \text{ bananas}} = \frac{\textbf{6} \text{ apples}}{\textbf{4} \text{ bananas}}$$

÷ 2

In the proportion above, three apples doubled would be six apples, and two bananas doubled would be four bananas. The fruit salad should taste the same whether the recipe is doubled or not, because the ratio of apples to bananas remains the same—3:2.

Equivalent ratios are sometimes written as proportions. To find equivalent ratios, first be sure to write them in the same order.

For example, if you wanted to mix up a deliciously tart apple-cranberry juice blend, you might use

two cups (473.2 mL) of apple juice for every **five cups** (1.83 L) of cranberry juice.

Suppose you see that you have 15 cups (3.55 L) of cranberry juice available, so you think about making more apple-cranberry juice blend. How many cups of apple juice would you need so that your juice blend tastes the same as the original recipe (or has the same ratio)?

You can set up this problem as a proportion to solve it (as seen below). Since 5 x 3 =15, then the 2 cups (473.2 mL) of apple juice need to be multiplied by 3 as well, to keep the same ratio. These are equivalent ratios, or proportions.

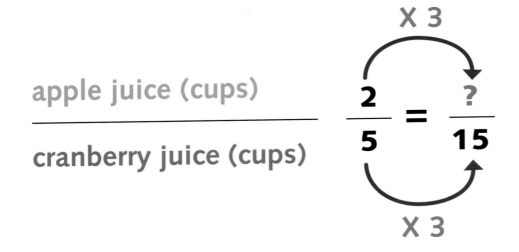

apple juice (cups)
─────────────────
cranberry juice (cups)

$$\frac{2}{5} = \frac{?}{15}$$

X 3

X 3

A proportion is the mathematical statement that two ratios are equal. If you write two equivalent ratios as fractions with an equal sign in between them, then you just wrote a proportion.

Try making some equivalent ratios (or proportions). Let the **"?"** stand for the unknown **quantity** that will make the ratios equivalent. Remember: First, find what the original ratio is multiplied by.

Then, apply that same multiplication rule to whichever part of the ratio has not yet been multiplied.

Practice A:

$$\frac{2}{3} = \frac{?}{12}$$

Practice B:

$$\frac{5}{6} = \frac{25}{?}$$

Another way of determining if ratios are equivalent is by comparing them in their simplest form. If their simplified **versions** are the same, then they are equivalent ratios. For example, if you want to **determine** if the following ratios are equivalent, you can compare their simplest forms.

COOK SERVE EA

THE GUIDE TO PERFECT seafood

The Country Cook

the Italian pasta book

Indian Cuisine

GOURMET. recipes

THE ORGANIC COOKBOOK

HOME COOKING

Baking: cakes & pastries

Traditional Recipes

Example:

Equivalent or not?

12 cookbooks for $84; 9 cookbooks for $63

$$\frac{\textbf{12 books}}{\textbf{\$84}} = \frac{\textbf{1 book}}{\textbf{\$7}} \qquad \frac{\textbf{9 books}}{\textbf{\$63}} = \frac{\textbf{1 book}}{\textbf{\$7}}$$

Both ratios are the same because their simplest forms are the same: $7 per cookbook or one cookbook for $7. This price per cookbook is also called a rate.

Rates and Unit Rates in the Grocery Store

A rate is a special type of ratio. It is a comparison of measurements that have different units, like dollars and minutes. Some real world examples of rates are found in your neighborhood grocery store.

The price of a bag of flour is $4.00 for a 10lb (4.54 kg) bag. That means the rate is $4/10lb ($4/4.54kg).

The price for a case of fresh avocados is $5.60 for 8 avocados. That means the rate is $5.60/8.

A unit rate (or unit price) is a rate with a **denominator** of 1. When you are shopping at the grocery store, many items are priced using unit rates. For example, if you go to the deli section, you will find meats and cheeses that are priced per pound.

Their unit prices will be: $3.20/lb (0.45 kg) of American cheese, $7.00/lb (0.45 kg) of smoked turkey, etc. These are unit prices because they simplify the rate of cost per several units to cost *per one unit*. Our previous example of $7 per cookbook was also an example of a unit rate.

Greek/Latin Roots in Math:

uni means one

cent means 100

equi means equal

graph means to write/draw

fract means break

div means separate

Let's try one together:
Write the rate as a unit rate.

$8 for 4 tomatoes

First, write the rate as a fraction.

$$\frac{\text{dollars}}{\text{tomatoes}} = \frac{\$8}{4 \text{ tomatoes}}$$

Then, since a unit rate is written with a one as the denominator, divide the denominator to get your goal of one on the bottom.

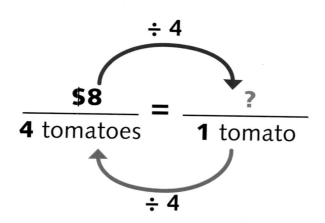

$$\frac{\$8}{4 \text{ tomatoes}} = \frac{?}{1 \text{ tomato}}$$

Finally, divide the **numerator** by the same number that you divided the denominator.

Whatever you do to the bottom, you have to do to the top (and **vice versa**).

Since $8 divided by four is $2, then the unit rate (or unit price) of each tomato is $2.

Try making some unit rates!

A. $\dfrac{6 \text{ miles}}{3 \text{ hours}} = \dfrac{?}{1 \text{ hour}}$ 　 B. $\dfrac{40 \text{ words}}{2 \text{ minutes}} = \dfrac{?}{1 \text{ minute}}$

C. $\dfrac{30 \text{ ice cubes}}{5 \text{ trays}} = \dfrac{?}{1 \text{ tray}}$

Answers:
A. 2 miles per hour   B. 20 words per minute   C. 6 ice cubes per tray

27

Percents are ratios too!

The Greek and Latin root *cent* means hundred, so percent means per 100. If you score an 80% on a 100-question test, then you answered 80 out of 100 questions correctly.

You don't need 100 questions to score an 80%, though. The rate of your correct answers is 80 per 100 (80/100). This means on a test with 25 questions, you answered 20 correctly out of 25 (20/25).

Ratios are everywhere! You just have to start looking. Who would have known that they were in your kitchen this whole time?

Glossary

comparison (kuhm-PAR-i-suhn): the activity or result of comparing

denominator (di-NAH-muh-nay-tur): the number in a fraction that is under the line and that shows how many equal parts the whole number can be divided into

determine (di-TUR-muhn): to make a discovery or to find out

equivalent (i-KWIV-uh-luhnt): the same in amount, value, or importance

numerator (NOO-muh-ray-tur): in fractions, the numerator is the number above the line. The numerator shows how many parts of the denominator are taken.

quantity (KWAHN-ti-tee): a number or amount

resulted (ri-ZUHLT-ed): caused by or happened because of something else

scrumptious (SKRUHMP-shus): very pleasant to taste

versions (VUR-zhuhns): different or changed forms of something such as a book or software

vice versa (VISE VUR-suh): a Latin phrase meaning the other way around

Index

Websites to Visit

www.mathplayground.com/ASB_RatioBlaster.html)

www.mathtv.com

www.mathsframe.co.uk

About The Author

Melanie Alvarez is a sixth grade mathematics teacher at an environmentally focused charter school in Florida. When she is not working as a teacher, private tutor, or writer, she enjoys spending time with her husband and two sons. Melanie is a firm believer in the power of reading and in raising her children and students to be lifelong learners.

Meet The Author!
www.meetREMauthors.com

www.rourkeeducationalmedia.com

PHOTO CREDITS: All images from Shutterstock. Cover: © Serbinka, brain/lightbulb © Positive Vectors; Page 4 © Keep Calm and Vector, page 5 © Monkey Business Images; page 6-7 © pornpoj, page 7 circle © In-Finity; page 9 © In-Finity; page 10 apple © monticello, bananas © someone, page 11 blackberries © Binh Thanh Bui, strawberries © Vasily Menshov, walnuts © Roman Baiadin, chocolate © Dieter Hahn; page 12 g Maksym Holovinov, page 13 cupcake © urfin, candies © Binh Thanh Bui; page 14 © Peangdao; pages 16-19 apple juice © Kryuchka Yaroslav, cranberry juice © Mtsaride; pages 20-21 © gfdunt; pages 22-23 grocery store © bikeriderlondon, flour © Paul Daniels, avocados © Nordling; pages 24-25 deli © Tyler Olson; pages 26-27 © MC_Noppadol; pages 28-29 © Serbinka

Edited by: Keli Sipperley

Cover and Interior design by: Nicola Stratford   www.nicolastratford.com

Library of Congress PCN Data

Ratios and Rates Reasoning / Melanie Alvarez
 (Math Masters: Analyze This!)
 ISBN 978-1-68191-734-4 (hard cover)
 ISBN 978-1-68191-835-8 (soft cover)
 ISBN 978-1-68191-928-7 (e-Book)
 Library of Congress Control Number: 2016932658

Rourke Educational Media
Printed in the United States of America, North Mankato, Minnesota

Also Available as:

ROURKE'S
e-Books